T0145024

STORIES and POEMS

Written from the Heart

By Substitute Teachers
In Alberta, Canada

WestBow Press books may be ordered through booksellers or by contacting:

WestBow Press
A Division of Thomas Nelson & Zondervan
1663 Liberty Drive
Bloomington, IN 47403
www.westbowpress.com
844-714-3454

ISBN: 978-1-6642-9710-4 (sc)
ISBN: 978-1-6642-9711-1 (e)

Print information available on the last page.

WestBow Press rev. date: 07/17/2023

DEDICATION

To anyone who has ever been a substitute teacher or ever will substitute teach, a toast to you! To teachers and non-teachers, may you enjoy this book. May you laugh and empathize with those who are in this noble profession. I began my teaching career in Bonnyville, Alberta, where I taught for seven years. In Calgary, I have over 2000 substitute teaching days to my credit. Currently, I am the Past Chair of the Calgary Public Substitute Teachers' Group Executive. Here I am with Anne Deeves on my left, a fellow substitute teacher with whom I was working with on the Executive. Here is our toast to all substitute teachers!

Karen Williams

ACKNOWLEDGEMENT OF THE LAND

The Alberta Teachers' Association acknowledges Treaty 4, 6, 7, 8 and 10 territories within Alberta. We acknowledge the many First Nations, Métis and Inuit whose footsteps have marked these lands for generations, including the many places that you are joining from. We are grateful for the traditional Knowledge Keepers and Elders who are still with us today and those who have gone before us. We recognize the land as an act of reconciliation and gratitude to those whose territory we reside on or are visiting.

L'Alberta Teachers' Association reconnait les territoires visés par les Traités nos 4, 6, 7, 8 et 10 situés en Alberta. Nous reconnaissons les nombreux membres des peuples des Premières Nations, les Métis et les Inuits dont les pas foulent ces terres, y compris les différents endroits à partir desquels vous vous joignez à nous, depuis des générations. Nous sommes reconnaissants envers les gardiens du savoir traditionnel et les Ainés, ceux qui sont toujours parmi nous comme ceux qui nous ont précédés. Nous reconnaissons ces terres en guise d'acte de réconciliation et pour exprimer notre gratitude envers ceux dont le territoire est l'endroit où nous résidons ou que nous visitons.

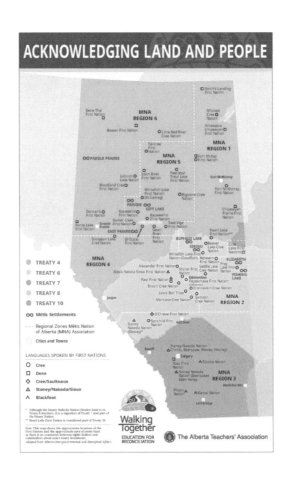

FOREWARD

I am a long-time advocate for substitute teachers. The unique circumstances which apply to substitute teachers make it a difficult and sometimes underappreciated job. Substitute teachers may be new university graduates looking for a permanent position, lifelong practitioners in the role of a substitute teacher, or retired classroom teachers who want to continue contributing to a career they love.

Substitute teachers are an integral part of the education system. They have the same certification requirements as other teachers and are full active members of the Alberta Teachers' Association. They have the same roles and responsibilities as any other classroom teacher. From one day to the next, substitute teachers are expected to teach a broad variety of subjects and multiple grade levels in different schools. Sometimes they teach in more than one school jurisdiction. This requires strong, general knowledge, flexibility, organization and a particular attitude to enable them to be successful in their craft.

The following collection of reflections, stories, poems, artwork and photographs form the basis of a tribute to substitute teachers in the province of Alberta. First envisioned in 2017 as a project to celebrate the 100th anniversary of the formation of the Alberta Teachers' Association (ATA), members of the Substitute Teachers' Group, Calgary Public Teachers', Local 38, have spent innumerable hours collecting artifacts for this publication. They have received contributions from throughout the province by substitute teachers and others to provide a unique and eclectic perspective into the service of substitute teachers. This is their life.

The contents of this collection will provide readers with some insight into the lives and work of substitute teachers. It is my hope that readers will gain a new appreciation for the collective contributions of substitute teachers over the past one hundred or so years. Enjoy.

Kevin Kempt
President (2016-2018)
Calgary Public Teachers, Local 38
Alberta Teachers' Association

THE INSPIRATION BEHIND THE STORIES AND POEMS
Marcheta Titterington

A few years ago, when the Alberta Teachers' Association (ATA) was celebrating its 100th Anniversary, I remember being inspired by the historical, archival articles that were published in the ATA News. Being the history buff that I am, I was again inspired when I attended as a delegate to the Annual Representative Assembly (ARA) of the Alberta Teachers' Association at that time. There we were told that there were 265 retired teachers 90 years of age and older, with the oldest lady being 108 and the oldest man being 101 years of age. I was in awe of their longevity. I thought it would be wonderful if their stories were told; if a family member or someone sat with them and recorded their stories about teaching or subbing in Alberta. I wondered what happened in small towns, in the one-room schoolhouse in years past. Who did they call upon when they were not able to teach on occasion; was it the farmer's wife or the hardware merchant's daughter? I wanted to know if Mary took her little lamb to school or maybe Johnny fell down the well when his teacher was not there to keep him in line. The next year when I attended the ARA as a delegate, we were told that the lady was now 109 years of age and that she had been collecting her pension for 45 years.

It was then I envisioned publishing a beautiful book of stories about substitute teaching in Alberta over the years. I decided to enlist the support of my close friend and substitute colleague, Penny Smith, whom I knew had been a journalist for some years. With the blessing of our Substitute Teachers' Group Executive Committee of the ATA, Local 38, in Calgary, Penny and I embarked on this amazing journey. I sent out press releases to the ATA News and the retired teachers' magazine News and Views inviting all Alberta teachers, retired teachers, and substitute teachers to be a part of history and share their memories and experiences about subbing over the years in Alberta.

So, our journey brings us to today. Our small Book Project Committee of two became a committee of six, and wonderful stories were written and sent in by teachers, retired teachers, and substitute teachers from all over Alberta, even from a retired teacher now living in British Columbia, who once subbed at a school in Northern Alberta. The stories range from the bittersweet to the hilarious. You'll have tears streaming down your face from laughter and you will surely see yourself in many of these stories.

Our COVID chapter became a part of our book by special request from our Substitute Teachers' Executive Committee. This chapter features very special poems that came to us over these past two years, along with beautiful pictures of quilts stitched, tapestries woven, and a picture painted.

ATA INTERVIEW WITH MARCHETA TITTERINGTON

Book project seeks stories about subbing
June 12, 2018, Jen Janzen, ATA News Staff

It was the ATA's 100th anniversary that got Marcheta Titterington thinking about the contributions that substitute teachers have made in the last 100 years.

A substitute teacher for her entire teaching career, Titterington, in conjunction with Calgary Public Local No. 38, is compiling stories from around the province that speak of the unique role substitute teachers play in the public education system. She, along with colleague Penny Smith, is seeking stories of substitute teaching from around the province for their compilation book, 100 Years of Subbing in Alberta.

"Over the course of the past year, archival stories were appearing in the ATA News, and it got me thinking," she explained. "There are so many stories around subbing in Alberta that could be told."

From a teacher who had to perform double duty as a midwife to a teacher standing in the pulpit to replace a parish priest, many interesting stories have already crossed Titterington's desk, and she's been happy to receive them.

According to the Alberta Teachers' Retirement Fund Board, there are 232 retired teachers in Alberta who are 95 and over. Of those, 28 retired members are older than 100. They have a unique perspective on teaching in Alberta and, Titterington says, there's a limited amount of time left to capture their memories.

"Once these older people have passed on, they'll take their stories with them," she said.

She points out that the group isn't seeking stories only from retired members. Teachers at any stage of their career can participate as long as their stories reflect the experience of substitute teachers.

"We want stories right up to the present," Titterington says.

"Maybe somebody else will write about the next 100 years."

Titterington herself graduated from university when she was 49 years old. Getting her teaching credentials was a lifelong dream.

"I'm really glad I took that leap, even at a later age," she said.

"It's been really rewarding over the years."

Now 74, Titterington is still teaching in Calgary classrooms from kindergarten to Grade 12.

"I still have energy and I love what I do, and I absolutely love what I do and the kids I teach. Why would I stop?"

ACKNOWLEDGEMENTS
Marcheta Titterington

It has been an amazing, incredible journey my dear friend and colleague, Penny Smith, and I embarked on in 2017. We have so many wonderful authors and contributors to thank for their input towards this beautiful book of stories, poems, and artwork.

First, I would personally like to thank Penny for all her invaluable support from the beginning in making this a reality today and for keeping me focused and accountable. I would also like to thank our other wonderful committee members: Karen Williams for her encouraging support, insight, gift for words and writing on our behalf, Marcia Hicks and Lee Nagy for their countless hours of work putting the manuscript of the book and pictures together, as well as editing, and Valsa Peter, our Communications Expert, for researching missing biographies, editing and always promoting our book. We have tried to keep the voice of each author as we edited for clarity, grammar, simplicity, length, and continuity. Submissions may not necessarily reflect the views of our Book Project Committee or that of the Publisher.

We wish to thank our Consulting Editor, Robert Benner, an English teacher with the Calgary Board of Education, and Bob Cocking, President of the ATA, Local 38, and Executive Staff Officer, Dan Nelles, for kindly advising and graciously editing for us also. Our deep appreciation and thanks to Stephen Cocking, Graphic Designer, for enhancing the layout of our book.

Our grateful thanks to Kevin Kempt, former president of the ATA, Local 38, who believed in our book project from the beginning and kindly wrote our Foreward. We truly appreciate permission given to us from the ATA for the Acknowledgement of the Land, the gracious support of the ATA Office Staff, and the generous financial support of the ATA, the Council of School Representatives, retired substitute teacher Bev Jaremko and substitute teacher Valsa Peter. We especially thank Nelson Moulton, Vice-President of Local 38, for going out on a limb for us, for which we will be forever grateful.

Our very special thanks to Cory Hare, Editor of the *ATA News,* and to Vi Oko, Editor of the Retired Teachers' magazine, *News and Views,* for kindly publishing our request for stories, and to Jen Janzen, *ATA News*, for interviewing me about our request for stories. We thank Cory Hare, also, for capturing a few Committee Members' biography pictures.

To our family and friends who supported us, we love you. To our very special authors, artists, and photographers, we are beyond grateful. Our heartfelt appreciation and thanks to you for your submissions. You indeed wrote from your hearts and bared your souls, lifted our spirits, blessed us with your memories, and made us laugh with your infectious humour. You showed us the importance of connections we have with the children and young people we teach and the difference we make when we are out subbing and teaching for the love of children.

TABLE OF CONTENTS

1

MEMORIES

A one-room schoolhouse on the Alberta prairie.

The One-Room Schoolhouse
Joyce Verrier

My mother, Stephania Lozinsky, went to school in Spedden, Alberta in the 1920s. It was a one-room school. The same teacher taught all grades because the area was sparsely populated. All students could hear everything being taught to all grades. My mother was a keen learner and paid close attention to everything being taught. As a result, she knew everything that was taught to all grades. There were no other teachers in the area and certainly no one to replace the teacher when he was unable to teach. When Mom was in Grade 3 (this would be 1927 or 1928), the teacher asked her if she would teach for him when he had to be absent. She successfully taught everything she was asked to do. Although she was only a grade three student, the teacher gave her credit for passing grade seven at the end of the year. The situation for my mother was excellent for two reasons: there was no school where they moved to and, at that time in history, grade seven was considered to be a high education. She had excellent skills in mathematics and language arts; well above the expected skill level of a grade three student. She was competent writing in both English and Ukrainian.

Mom always wished she could have had the opportunity to become a teacher and often spoke of the days she taught at Spedden. With the record she had from Spedden, it would not have taken much more training for her to become a teacher, but life didn't present her with the opportunity. Mom gave life to seven children. This took up all her time and all available money, so she had no opportunity to fulfill her dreams. When I decided to become a teacher, Mom was very happy – perhaps a small link to the career she wanted.

I will say I am extremely grateful for the opportunities I had in life. I taught in several venues including colleges, middle and high schools, youth detention centers, jails, Native Reserves, and a Métis Settlement school, as well as developing learning resources for Alberta Learning. The nicest thing now about my career is that I am in my 70s and can substitute teach. I have no grandchildren. The students at school are my surrogate grandchildren. I love interacting with them and look forward to each day I can spend with them. I have been working with Métis children in ECS to Grade 8 since my retirement sixteen years ago. It is this interaction with youth that helps me keep feeling young and enjoying my "golden years."

I regret I have no pictures of the school or my mother at that time. Money was extremely scarce, few people had cameras, and so the records are limited.

"How Did You Get So Old?"
Marcheta Titterington

I was only four years of age when I started kindergarten at a big old sandstone school in northwest Calgary, King George School, in 1948. Calgary was a small city then, with country-like roads and no shopping centres (except for downtown), but we did have grocery stores and smaller corner grocery stores. I remember chocolate bars were only five cents in those days.

My mom, dad and I, until my brother John came along, lived on a chicken farm in the community of Mount Pleasant, about seven or eight blocks from King George School. Over the years I have loved going back to teach there and sharing with the younger children and the older students, tidbits each time, about what life was like when I came to their school as a little girl a long time ago. They are fascinated by the olden days. I tell them about the cows grazing near our chicken farm which today is called Confederation Park. Life was simpler then, not busy like it is today, and the old cars did not drive very fast.

Parents did not drive you to school in those days, and they usually did not walk you to school except for the first day. Moms maybe cried that first day because they were losing their babies starting kindergarten. You might have cried too because it was a new beginning at a very large school. The little six-year-old boy who lived across the country road from us, Tommy, would walk me back and forth to school. We walked no matter the weather, even in the wintertime.

Not everyone had a telephone in Calgary in those days, and so the few neighbours near us had to come over to our place to use the phone. There were no televisions, no computers, no cell phones, no iPads, no favourite fast-food restaurants, and no favourite toy stores.

"What?" the children asked. "How did you live?"

Well, we did not know any differently because all those things, like computers, favourite toy stores, and fast-food restaurants, came later. They were not part of our little world at the time. We had radios, though, which our parents listened to. As children, girls played with their dolls and boys played with their toy cars, trucks and trains. Outdoors, we rode bikes or pushed dolly carriages, played hopscotch, marbles or jacks, and tobogganed and skated in the winter. We always had fun playing at a nearby park with our friends or swimming in a swimming pool, especially at an outdoor pool in warmer weather.

Earlier this spring, 2021, I was again subbing at King George School for a kindergarten class in the morning and a dance class in the Learning Commons in the afternoon. I told my kindergarten children how I came to their school for kindergarten, too, when I was only four years of age. I also told a Grade 1 class that day about coming to their school. The next time I had that same class, one of the little boys sweetly said to me, "I have a question for you."

"Okay," I said. "What is your question?"

He looked up at me with inquisitive eyes and asked, "How did you get so old?"

"I don't know," I said. "You know that I came here for kindergarten when I was a little girl, and Tommy, the little boy who lived across the country road from us, walked me to school and back home each day. Then I went to Grades 1 and 2 and 3 and all the way to Grade 12. I went to work, and you know I married Tommy and we had four children. I went to college and then university and became a teacher. Our children grew up and they had children of their own, and I guess the years just went by, and now I'm a great-grandma with sixteen grandchildren, the last time I counted, and eight great-grandchildren. *Imagine that!*"

My little grade-one friend seemed to understand, in his own way, how I got so old. I thanked him for asking me, before he went back to class with his friends and before I greeted my next dance class.

Marcheta (age 4) and Tommy (age 6) with their new gifts, Christmas 1948.

Growing Up in the Olden Days
Mara Ganten

I was subbing in a Grade 3 classroom for the day. I was outside doing recess supervision and one of my grade-three students came up to me and asked if she could hold my hand while I was walking. So, we were walking hand-in-hand and chatting, and she asked me, "What was it like growing up in the olden days?"

I smiled and quietly chuckled to myself. When I think of the "olden days," I think of the time before vehicles and electricity – back when we had horses and carriages and no running water. But, before I responded, "I wouldn't really consider my childhood as growing up in the olden days," I thought about my answer.

"Well, we didn't have the internet until I was in Grade 10. We used to have computer class once a week when we were in elementary school. The computers were huge white boxes with black and green screens. We had to turn the computers on half an hour before class started to give them enough time to power up and start working. The only game we could play was Oregon Trail. It was a game where you started out in a wagon on the Oregon Trail, and you had to make it through a series of experiences, like losing your food or getting bitten by a snake. The only other thing we ever did on computers was typing practice. We didn't really have cell phones. Only really important business people seemed to have cell phones. I didn't get a cell phone until I was in university. We didn't have DVDs or movie screens in our vehicles."

The grade-three student listened intently to me and couldn't believe how different things were. Initially, I thought the question was hilarious because I don't consider the '80s and '90s as the olden days. Plus, it made me stop and think about how much things have changed since I was a kid.

Bittersweet
Linda Klym

My husband had taught in Ardrossan Elementary School for 30 years. They even named the gym after him when he retired. His last year of teaching was my daughter's first year of teaching in the same school. She taught kindergarten and they really enjoyed seeing each other in the hallway or staffroom. My daughter's teaching career was cut short when she was diagnosed with a brain tumour. She died before I started being a substitute teacher. I subbed in Ardrossan often, even though the first few times were painful for me. I could see so many reminders of my husband and my daughter: the kindergarten classroom, the gym with my husband's picture above the doors, and my husband's old office. The best reminder was the staff and students. The staff had many memories of both my husband and daughter that they shared with me. My students would tell me what great teachers they were. The worst was when a rather unruly student in Grade 6 yelled out, "Hey, aren't you the mom of that teacher that died?" Some of the more considerate students chastised his rudeness and I barely got through that class without crying. (The tears came later.)

A small footnote. My husband died in 2017. He never really got over the death of his daughter. So, all three of us had participated in Ardrossan School: my husband who spent most of his career there, my daughter who was so proud to be a young teacher starting out, and me, a substitute teacher. It is sad to say that the school has been shut down and demolished (not sure if all of it is gone now). A new school stands in its place. The gym has become a parking lot and the sign over the door saying the Klym Gym is now in my basement, along with all the other memories of so many years of teaching.

You never know what life holds for you and what is just around the corner. What I do know is that teaching, both regular and substitute, was the best part of my life. It is truly one of the best professions and I was honoured to be called "Teacher."

Accidents Happen
Mara Ganten

On my first day as a substitute, one of my students had a bad accident. I was teaching kindergarten and we were playing in the gym. Two students ran head-on into each other. They were both looking over their shoulders behind them and didn't see the other coming. One kid was crying hysterically, and the other little girl was sort of whimpering a little.

I said, "Oh, it looks like you bit your tongue. It's not that bad." All the while I am looking at the Educational Assistant (EA) and mouthing the words, "It's *really* bad." This girl was so brave. The EA took her into the bathroom, and she gently washed her mouth out. She had bitten right through her tongue. It was almost the end of the day, so she just waited in the office until her parents came to get her. I dismissed the class at the end of the day and went to sit with her until someone came to pick her up. I was sort of nervous that her parents would be upset with me because their little girl got hurt. Boy, was I wrong!

Her dad arrived and I found out he was a doctor. He wasn't upset at all. As a matter of fact, he asked if we had a suture kit so he could just put in a few quick stitches right there in the office. I informed him that no, we didn't have a suture kit and she would have to go to the clinic or hospital. All the while I am thinking, I know this girl is tough, but shouldn't she receive an anesthetic before Dad starts stitching her tongue up? Thankfully, as we didn't have a suture kit on hand, he had to take her to the clinic to have it done!

A Truly Special Day
James Baker

Prior to the 2010 Vancouver Winter Olympics, I had an incredible substitute teaching experience! It was a winter morning in January 2010, and I had a last-minute call from the SEMS System asking me to take a job in the northwest part of Calgary. I accepted, but I worried about the length of time it would take to arrive during a winter morning storm.

Travelling across the city, I arrived at the school and made it to the classroom. There, I was told I would be accompanying several classes on a field trip to the Olympic Oval at the University of Calgary! The last of the speed skating trials for the 2010 Canadian Olympic team were occurring at the Oval. The students and teachers would meet two qualifying speed skaters and the official life-size Olympic Mascots Miga and Quatchi. I had a spectacular visit and a truly special day with my students.

Crabby Patty
James Baker

At one of my favourite junior high schools, I had a special visitor join us. She had hitched a ride to school in the pack of one of the girls, with a boost from a mischievous brother. As students were doing their humanities lesson, I circulated the room. To my astonishment, there was a very learned Hermit crab in front of me on the student's desk.

"Her name is Crabby Patty," she replied. "I found her in my pack!"

Crabby Patty made it back to her private locker for the rest of the day and lived on to tell her tale at home.

The German Shepherd
Penny Smith

I was subbing in a Grade 3 class at an elementary school and there was a Show and Tell in the afternoon. At recess I had a student, who was an ESL learner from the former Yugoslavia, ask me if he could show his dog in the afternoon. I asked what kind of dog he had but he could not tell me. I said yes to the student, being partial to dogs as I had a beautiful Golden Retriever at home.

At lunchtime, his dad came to see me to tell me the dog was big. It was a German Shepherd, and the dad would be there with the dog.

There were certainly gasps from some of the girls, as the dog was a *huge* German Shepherd. The Show and Tell did go well.

Another memorable Show and Tell was at another school when a mother showed a boa constrictor.

These two Show and Tell times stand out for me as the German Shepherd dog was certainly beautiful and well-behaved. Despite his size, the dog was not aggressive. The dad would have had to go through the volunteer evaluation in these days. The mother, who brought in the snake, was also very calm with it. Again, the snake was huge. I was also feeling a little scared, but the mother had the permission of the school's principal.

These two Show and Tells certainly stand out for me in my subbing career.

We Are Turning Good for You
Kathy Cook

My first experience as a substitute teacher started out like a scene from one of those zany, painfully uncomfortable, situation comedies. You know, the ones where you console yourself by thinking this is really awful, but it will seem hilarious years from now. On day one, the class of sweet little darlings seemed to morph into a room full of mischievous, taunting elves. As the first paper wads sailed through shrieks of laughter, it became increasingly clear there were two choices to be made. Learn effective ways to control classroom situations or choose another career. Panic-stricken, that evening I phoned the two seasoned educators that I knew, Benny Cook, my brother, and Norma Macintosh, a good friend and colleague. Notepad in hand I frantically jotted down scads of their tried-and-true skills and techniques. For the next few weeks, Benny and Norma were kind enough to take me under their wings and encourage me to keep them on speed dial.

Eventually, I began to find myself looking forward to the more challenging groups of students. The effectiveness of my newly acquired ability to keep students orderly, focused and attentive truly hit home when I went to the staff room, at a school where I was subbing, and the teachers at the school asked me how things were going. When I said everything was fine, they looked both shocked and surprised. At the end of the week, one of the students handed me a note that said, "We are turning good for you."

After working as a full-time teacher for over two decades, I have retired. Now, at the end of the full circle, from subbing to homeroom teacher and back to subbing again, I realize in hindsight, Benny and Norma's teaching advice was rooted in the provision of opportunities to meet students' needs and to encourage their successes, versus illuminating their mistakes and failures. From ages three to ninety-three, all people wish to feel valued and appreciated.

I will be forever grateful to these two kind souls, Benny and Norma, who took the time to share their wisdom and knowledge.

And yes, those first few days of teaching were indeed awful, and yes, upon reflection, they do seem hilarious now.

Lockdown for Dessert
Shirley Ewing

Lockdown drills are a regular part of the school year to ensure that everyone is prepared and knows what to do in the event of an emergency. As a substitute, I often said that I thought the schools must schedule their drills to coincide with me being in a particular location. I was present for enough drills that I had the routine memorized, right down to what the police would say to us when they entered the room.

One day I went into a foods class feeling particularly tired. There had been multiple challenges in the morning with weather, traffic, and classroom management issues. I looked out the window at the swirling snow and thought that it was just the kind of day to have a fire alarm. I knew it would not be a scheduled drill in that weather, yet it was a Murphy's Law kind of day.

As I dealt with student questions and complaints, I reminded myself to let go of the stress that came as students displayed immaturity due to their age, and other not-so-excusable reasons. Suddenly, I heard that there was an announcement but could not make out what was said.

One of the girls in the corner kitchen exclaimed, "It's a lockdown!"

My immediate thought was, "Of course, it is." And I may have expressed my thoughts out loud.

No one had prepared me for a potential drill that morning, and I was not looking for excitement. Two or three students hurried into the room and pulled the door shut behind them. Someone turned the lights out at one end of the room, as I quickly inventoried all the possible noises in the room that could alert an intruder to our presence there. Some of the ovens were preheating, and one student begged me not to turn them off as they already had something baking in them. Thinking that it would probably not be an issue, I quickly checked each stove to ensure that no timers had been set. Then I turned out the last light which was awkwardly located at the opposite end of the room from the rest.

I sunk to the floor out of sight of the door, where the whole class was crowded into a single kitchen unit to wait out whatever danger, or imaginary danger, lurked outside of the room. Hardly a reminder was required to keep the students seated silently for the next several minutes. Then one of the girls very quietly expressed concern at the prospect that, if the lockdown continued past a certain point, their pumpkin pie might be spoiled. We watched the clock anxiously. When the time came, they whispered the question regarding what they should do.

Carefully and in near silence I instructed the two girls that they could go to the oven and rescue the pie on the condition that they do it silently and stay below the counter level. Taking my instructions particularly seriously, I raised my eyebrows as both girls laid down and slithered across the dusty floor on their bellies. Not a speedy way to cross in front of the door, but at least I was assured that they were listening to my instructions.

This triggered several other students to whisper concerns about food that was on their counters, waiting to be cooked, that could not be successfully saved for another day. Checking how long was needed and trying to express the same conditions and expectations, I agreed that the remaining items could be put in the ovens for cooking. There was an instant flurry of activity while no less than four young people leapt from the floor and flew across the classroom to their workspaces. Frantically, I waved my arms in a silent plea for them to get down below waist height.

It was to this silent, chaotic scene that my heart sank at the simultaneous appearance of the police at our door. I braced myself for the inevitable corrections and warnings that were sure to follow. But they never came. The constable simply reassured us that all were safe and asked us to wait until the announcement. Then he went his way, leaving me staring at the closed door in disbelief. The class rose from their positions on the floor and dutifully went to work finishing responsibilities and cleaning the classroom.

The rest of the day proceeded in a relatively ordinary manner, aside from the necessary impromptu staff meeting at lunch. Not desiring to be too conspicuous, I sat quietly listening to all that was said. Along with a brief explanation of what had happened and instructions for what to do in the event of any related problems, thanks were expressed to all for their prompt and accurate responses to the incident. The principal was careful to mention her appreciation for the way the subs – and there were a significant number of subs – had responded, as well. As a final comment, turning to me in the presence of everyone, she announced, "The police said your room smelled great!"

My Life in Three Avatars
Valsa Peter

This is my teaching saga set in three countries: India, Saudi Arabia, and Canada...in other words, three incarnations!

You must have all heard or seen the movie *Avatar. Avatar*, Sanskrit "avatāra" (descent), in Hinduism, is the incarnation of a deity in human or animal form to counteract some evil in the world. This is the meaning I have chosen for my story. You see, I am from India, where I was born and brought up for the first thirty-odd years of my life. Sanskrit is the mother language of most Indian languages. Even as you are reading this you will understand my love of languages and learning! I believe that language, music, food, and art are the foundational stones of all cultures.

So, growing up in India – what can I say? So vastly different then from India today: no computers, no electronic devices, and no large manufacturing companies. Agriculture was our mainstay and family life was our bond. Education and learning were particularly important parts of our lives. As a little girl, I started my school in a Catholic convent run by nuns – very disciplined, highly conventional. My first career choice was journalism and, even though I was accepted into a highly prestigious school of journalism, my family convinced me it was not an appropriate choice for a girl! However, teaching was a good career for a girl, especially when it came to marriage. You must be wondering Hmm! Why is that? Well, in those days, arranged marriages were the only way to enter the marital world. One of the advantages of being a teacher was being at home during the holidays with the children. So, I was encouraged by my parents to choose a teaching career. Marriage in those days was the be-all and end-all of a girl's life!

However, my dad was a very liberal and forward-thinking gentleman. I was born after three sons and was the only daughter. According to custom, it was only after I got married that my siblings could get married. But my dad insisted that I graduate with a teaching degree and have the financial means to be independent before I got married. This was quite a radical departure from the way people thought in those days. My dad instilled in me this saying, "Your bread should be in your hands." In other words, if I were financially independent and earning my own money, no one could subjugate me or treat me badly. My education would give me the economic independence to be an equal partner in a marriage. So, I graduated with a Master's in Languages and a Degree in Education. But it was only after my two children were born that I started teaching.

Teaching in India in those days was quite different. India from time immemorial had a strong educational system based on the teacher (guru) in charge, who was the mentor, guide, and leader. Students were shishyas and lived with the guru in his house. But after the British took over our educational system, we had the British school model. Discipline, structure, classwork and "chalk and talk" were the norms. "Why?", "Why not?", "What?" and "What if?" questions from students were never heard. It was not inquiry-based, as is the system in North America.

Teachers taught from textbooks with hardly any pictorial images. All lessons were written on the chalkboard. It was the student's responsibility to copy everything from the board and memorize large portions. By the time our students completed Grade 1, they could repeat the times tables from one to sixteen, count to 1000, and read and write English and the local vernacular language. Poems ranging from Shakespeare's sonnets to modern-day classics, like Robert Frost's *A Road Not Taken,* and quotes from the Bhagavad-Gita, Thirukural (literature from Indian languages) were part of our memorization itinerary!

Class sizes were large. How large you ask? About fifty to sixty in a class. I remember teaching a class of about seventy-plus students one time. This class was quite large and there were large windows at the back of the class, backing onto the playground. The windows were open most of the time. So, I was writing on the board, which was the traditional vehicle used to teach in those days, and when I finished, I looked back at the class. Several youngsters were missing from the backbenches. After I explained what I had written, I turned back to the board to write some more stuff, completed it, and faced the class again. Surprise! The missing culprits were now back in their seats... but a new lot was missing!

Like here in elementary classes, the same teacher taught all the subjects. In high school, teachers rotated teaching various subjects. I was an English and Geography-cum-History teacher (social studies).

Loads of homework each day to correct. All handwritten. Marks to be entered in a long accounting-type logbook each night. Most students were regular in submitting their homework each day. Homework was a must! It was not only work that was incomplete but new work. In fact, parents were not happy if the teacher did not assign homework. Most schools had a general assembly each morning when we gathered in front of the school, sang our national anthem, and read short passages from the different religious books in the country. It was followed by the day's announcements and a short speech by the headmaster/headmistress.

So, by now you are thinking – what a dull boring life! No, not at all! Respect for teachers was instilled into the students. Parents constantly came to the school to inquire about their darlings' progress. Teachers and students had a great rapport. Being a small city, teachers also knew most of the parents. The Phys Ed. or Drill classes were a lot of fun. The weather being generally warm and sunny provided many opportunities for sports, especially football and cricket. Teachers used to meet in the staffroom after school and discuss a lot of issues. And always there was plenty of food in the staffroom… which I find is a common factor around the world. We also had clubs for various subjects like drama, music, arts, math, etc. I genuinely enjoyed my teaching days in the small town I lived in. The school was just behind my ancestral home and about ten steps away.

I thought this would be my life… I will work as a teacher, retire, collect my pension, and live happily ever after. *But ...*

This time I surfaced in Saudi Arabia in my next Avatar! My hubby was hired to work in a multinational oil company, so we all flew over to the Kingdom of Saudi Arabia and made an entirely new kind of life. Since this company was founded in the USA, we had our first taste of the American way of life. Our kids were enrolled in a school with an American curriculum. For the first time, I saw textbooks and workbooks with beautiful pictures and images. The whole teaching methodology was so different. I heard about inquiry pedagogy and fell in love with it! However, since I did not have an American teaching certification, I could not work in the school. So, I did the next best thing. I applied and got a job in the same company as my husband and the job was in the Education Department. You see, the company hired young Saudi men and women and enrolled them in training programs – academic and job skills. I became a training coordinator which involved interviewing and planning their future educational advancement. So, I was not actually teaching but was still involved in learning about the educational system in this capacity. Most of the new hires had already completed their schooling in the Saudi system. But when they were hired, they were enrolled in the company schools. Each one of them had a Professional Learning Program Plan. You can say it was akin to a guidance counsellor's job. It was part of my job description to help them choose the subjects and path that most suited the job for which they were hired, write the plan, review it, and keep up with their training goals. I enjoyed this new career path which brought new insights and understanding to this new culture. I came to know and reflect on the lives they lived. I learned a smattering of the Arabic language. What a culturally rich language!

Did you know that our English word "zero" comes from the Arabic word "sifr?" It is the same Arabic root that gives us "cipher" which can mean "empty" or "something is done in secret." We lived and worked in Saudi Arabia for about twenty-plus years. In the meantime, family life went full steam ahead. Both our children graduated from school (Grade 9) and went on to complete their high school and higher secondary education in the USA. *But …*

This time I surfaced in Canada in my latest Avatar! Since both my children wanted to live in the USA and we were not too keen to live there, we did the next best thing. We applied for Canadian immigration and *"Voila"* in a year's time we came to this marvelous, wonderful country. Once here my hubby went to work in the oil and gas industry. However, I decided I would go back to my first love. Teaching! I enrolled at the University of Calgary and completed my Bachelor of Education degree. (Now remember, I was no spring chicken!) I remember walking into the classroom and looking around. Most of the students, and even my professors, were younger than me. I adopted the Alberta pedagogical system as my own; yet kept some parts of my methodology from India in a back compartment of my brain – as a backup maybe? I discovered that asking questions and discussing issues was a highly active component of my new education. Learning here was not only writing endless essays, but also involved multiple choice, true/false, projects, artwork, presentations, seminars, and other creative methods to achieve my goals.

After I graduated, I worked the required number of days for certification and became a fully certified teacher in Alberta. Goal achieved! Now I was ready, willing and all set to start my new career and hopefully my last. At about the same time, I became a Canadian citizen too. I still remember the day my Permanent Certificate arrived in the mail!

I started my teaching career in Alberta, by working in a couple of private schools for a few years. Then I heard about the substitute teaching system in the Calgary Board of Education. I checked it out and found that I would be better off professionally and personally if I became a substitute teacher. So here I am. I am what I like to call a Sub Sandwich. This means I am a substitute with many fillings all the way from kindergarten to Grade 12. When the kids call out, "We have a sub," I tell them, "Yes, but a Sub Sandwich," and explain the meaning!

My initial area was elementary grades, and I thoroughly enjoyed my time in those classes. But as the years flew by, I started teaching in junior high and high schools. For one thing, I was getting older (not wiser), and the young ones were too full of energy. However, one thing is the same whether they are in Grade 1 or 12. I have to remind them to write their name before handing in their assignments.

I am now in my last and final Avatar! Hopefully, I will be in it until I decide to call it a day. I feel my teaching days are fulfilling and rewarding. I realize that teaching comes from the heart. I am aware of what Canada can provide...

a. There is security for all individuals irrespective of nationality, gender, race, etc.
b. Women have the same opportunities as men.
c. Freedom of speech and ideas are especially important in Canada.
d. Cultural diversity is provided for each of us.
e. Each student has the opportunity to first identify oneself as a person with freedoms: to learn, work, and choose life partners and lifestyles.

But most importantly, I can deliver learning with all its learning outcomes combined with important cultural values. This is especially important for young folk from traditional Asian countries as they shift to a western country. I can identify what are positive values and can choose the ones most suited for their individual chosen lifestyle. Again and again, I tell all my students, especially the girls, "Your bread is in your hands." (My "mantra" from my dad.)

I love teaching social studies and language arts. I compare the society here with other continents I have lived on. I compare the English language with other languages in my life as Avatars past! I am proud to change and relate to the ever-evolving curriculum substitutes present each day. To achieve this goal, I try to attend at least a couple of professional development seminars a year. During the past COVID year, my students and I discussed what this time means for each of us. We explored new ways of presenting ideas and projects, through poems, art, and music (of course, spelling is still important!) Skype and Zoom! We infused a new meaning to the old saying, "When life gives you lemons, ... you make the best lemonade ever!"

I am hoping that the inclusion of this story of my life will have a positive and comprehensive impact on all readers. Wishing each of my readers every success in whichever Avatar they are in now. Each Avatar in my life has only added value. Thanks for reading.

Valsa

2

LESSONS LEARNED

Labyrinth Walk
Marcia Hicks

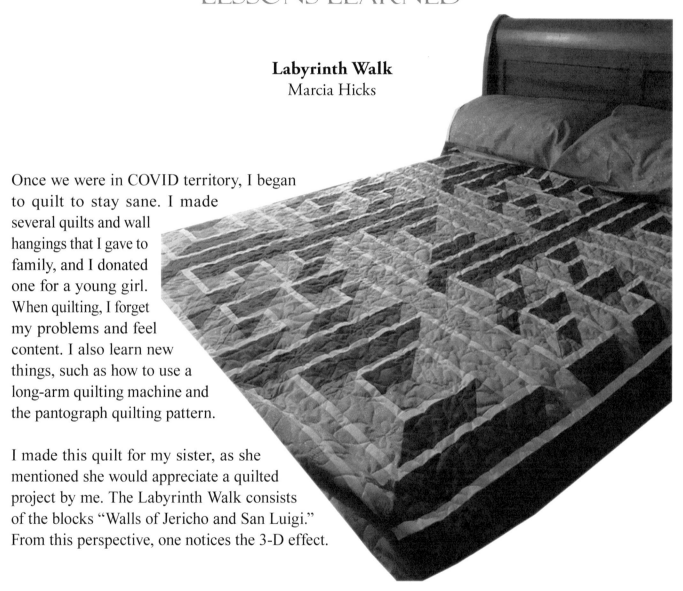

Once we were in COVID territory, I began to quilt to stay sane. I made several quilts and wall hangings that I gave to family, and I donated one for a young girl. When quilting, I forget my problems and feel content. I also learn new things, such as how to use a long-arm quilting machine and the pantograph quilting pattern.

I made this quilt for my sister, as she mentioned she would appreciate a quilted project by me. The Labyrinth Walk consists of the blocks "Walls of Jericho and San Luigi." From this perspective, one notices the 3-D effect.

When I Grow Up
Karen Williams

What do you want to be when you grow up? That is the question you often hear asked. I bet being a substitute teacher was never on your Top Ten list. Some of you are feeling guilty already. I bet you are remembering the stories you, your brother or sister, or a friend told about your substitute teacher. I bet never in your fondest dreams did you want to become a substitute teacher.

It was never on my Top Ten list either and here I am – working as a substitute teacher. I've been a substitute and temporary contract teacher for thirty years. Some teachers get a full-time teaching contract. Not me – I just stayed as a substitute and temporary contract teacher. Maybe I haven't impressed the principals that much when I've been a substitute teacher, especially during my early years.

For instance, I remember when I was locked out of the classroom. It was a Grade 5/6 classroom and, halfway through the morning, somehow the students were inside the room, and I was outside. There I was standing in the hall rattling the doorknob – "Let me in!"

The principal walked by and asked, "Anything wrong, Mrs. Williams?"

"No," I said, "I'm just standing in the hallway and watching the paint dry." I grinned embarrassingly. Of course, the students never did let me in. So, the principal opened the door and let me in the room. Not too impressive.

Then there was the time I had a student jump out the window. All I said was, "Take out your math book." He opened the window and was gone. I had to phone down to the office and say, "A student just climbed out the window."

Of course, the principal asked, "Why?"

I said, "I guess he just doesn't like math." That didn't work out too well with impressing a principal, either.

I haven't been too impressive at the high school level either. I'm an elementary teacher. The first time I was teaching high school, I had to take a class of thirty students to the library. So, just like in elementary, I lined them up at the door and led the way to the library. I got to the library, turned around and there were fifteen students.

The librarian asked, "Where's the rest of the class?"

I turned to a student near the back of the line and wailed, "Where did everyone go?"

He said, "Out for a walk, to buy some food, to the bathroom – they're gone."

So, I had to phone down to the office and say, "I just lost fifteen students." I never did see them for the rest of the morning. Not too impressive.

Another time I fell asleep in the classroom. I was substitute teaching for the resource teacher. When you're subbing for someone who doesn't have a regular class, the principal assigns you to cover different classes. The principal sent me to help in a Grade 1 classroom while she figured out where she would assign me for the day. The Grade 1 teacher was in the midst of reading the students a story in the story corner. He was a young first-year teacher. He asked the students to lie down on the story corner rug, close their eyes and imagine the story. It was a Friday afternoon and I had had a full week of half-day substitute teaching jobs. I closed my eyes and was so tired that I fell asleep and was out like a light. I was snoring away. Fifteen minutes later, the principal comes in with my assignment. By this time, the students had gone back to their desks and there I was – still snoring in the story corner. The teacher didn't know what to do with me. So, he just let me sleep.

The principal had to wake me up. She said, "I sure caught you sleeping on the job."

Of course, a little boy in the back added to my embarrassment by saying, "She was snoring so loud I couldn't even hear the Winnie the Pooh story." Again, not too impressive.

Being a substitute teacher was never on my Top Ten list. However, I've developed some new strategies to stay one step ahead of the students. If the students try to lock me out, I now carry a key in my pocket. If I don't have a key, I will just go for coffee in the staffroom instead of standing in the hallway. If a student tries to jump out a window, I will be right behind. The rest of the students can do self-directed learning while I take a walk to calm down. Instead of leading the class down the hallway, I will follow at the end and maybe I can get lost instead of the students. Finally, the next time I'm sent to another classroom to wait, I'll ask the teacher to read an action story, so I stay awake.

The main thing I have learned as a substitute teacher is to think ahead of the students and, if you make a good impression and be a bit more impressive, just maybe when you grow up, you can get your dream job of being a teacher with a continuous teaching contract.

My First Day of Subbing
Roger Scott

My arm shot out for the receiver as the bedroom phone startled me at 6:25 am. A vaguely familiar voice queried through the foggy darkness, "Could you go to Lorne Akins to sub today?"

Despite teaching, coaching, and serving as Assistant Principal and Principal at Lorne Akins Jr. High in St. Albert, now retired, I smiled as I detected a wee touch of nervousness about me whilst I cleaned up and grabbed my lunch on the way out the door. What could possibly happen that I hadn't seen before?

Well, for one thing, my heartbeat rose steeply as I attempted to compete with parents, other substitutes, service trucks, cabs, school buses, city transport and a few other vehicles all vying for the two or three available parking spots within shouting distance of the building – no reserved parking for me anymore!

Next, I had to offer up usernames and passwords I had never heard of before and sign the appropriate substitute forms before getting my keys, class lists, attendance sheets, daily announcements, lesson plans, and special instructions for the day. All these came from an amazingly well-organized secretary, who was a multi-tasking super-star answering phone calls, dealing with parents across the counter, greeting and organizing all the teachers and subs, and filling the administrators in on just who was waiting for them in their offices.

Time for a coffee! I knew where the old machine was, and I still have one of my old mugs in the cupboard… but wait … the new-fangled coffee pot was empty! I could certainly make a simple pot of java, couldn't I? After all, a few short months ago I was an administrator in this building. Well, it wasn't two minutes before I had water running all over the counter and floor in the staffroom, coffee grounds roasting on the burner, and vast rolls of somewhat non-absorbent paper towels spread out protecting everyone's lunches, purses, marking, and plan books.

Smooth move and my mug was still empty!

Lingering a bit (to prevent any leering), I checked out my assignment and was a bit surprised to see that I was a TA today – in charge of the library no less... the same library that was always open a good fifteen minutes early. I hurriedly hung up my coat, grabbed my backpack, and fought teenage hallway traffic all the way to the library where the lights were on, students were working, reading, on computers, and visiting politely. Someone had seen me mopping up my caffeine disaster and was kind enough to open it for the students. Thank you!

I won't go into detail about the rest of the day other than to say I was one tired puppy by three o'clock. Who knew that this job was truly a theme on variations? Books, computers, supplies, teacher requests, student issues, lockdown drills, continuous interruptions, and a new-fangled system of digital magic for keeping track of all these vital resources. But I was a determined rookie and vowed to keep up with the rising tide of books that kept falling into the return slot.

By home time, I believe I had shelved close to one hundred books and was feeling even a tad smug about my accomplishments. Suddenly, at the end of the day, who should appear at the library counter but the regular librarian, smiling and relaxed after a day of in-service and quiet conversation. "How'd you make out here today?"

I lied quite naturally and said I had had a smooth and fabulous day, shelving at least a hundred books to really save her some time.

"Awesome," she purred. "Oh, by the way, you did check in all those titles using the scanner before you shelved the books, didn't you?"

They haven't asked me to work in the library since.

How to Resolve a Fight Without a Word
Karen McKenzieSmith

In my eleven years of subbing in Calgary, Alberta, I have encountered three or four fights, which I have had to deal with.

Technically teachers, such as myself, are not to get in the middle of any fights. However, I have found this technique to be 100% successful in dealing with actual fights, where fists are flying, and anger is escalated.

My technique is not something I would recommend everyone try. I especially think it would not work for a male teacher to utilize.

Believe it or not, this is what I do. I go over to the fight looking like I am trying to break it up. But I don't do that. What I do, in fact, is pretend one of them has accidentally hit me and knocked me out cold. Hence, I fall to the floor as if I'm knocked out by a hit. Not a real one, of course!

There's usually someone in the crowd who yells out, "You hit the teacher! You hit the teacher!"

This causes the two that are in a furious brawl to stop abruptly and tend to me, the teacher.

Once that happens, I come to and exclaim, "It's fine. I'm OK. Don't worry about it. Let's just get back to class."

Voila! The fight is over! All is resolved without a word directed at anyone. Everyone, especially the two that were fighting, has saved face and the fight, for whatever they were fighting for, is over and dealt with. No having to go outside behind the school to finish it off later.

Like I've said before, I would not recommend this. I am just saying that it was a technique that worked fabulously for me when I tried it – especially since it resolved the issue between the two who were fighting so magnificently. You see, neither one lost the fight *and* they both *won!*

My Early Subbing Days
Penny Smith

I had worked as a newspaper journalist, worked in the oil patch, and taught adult English as a Second Language (ESL) learners in Calgary when I decided to return to substitute teaching as I had thought there would be more opportunities to have a full-time teaching position.

I was used to teaching ESL adults, so I was a little nervous about teaching Grade 1. A former mentor teacher, who supervised me when I was getting my diploma in ESL, asked if I would sub for her. I dutifully read the lesson and planned my day.

The class seemed to be going well, but suddenly during mid-morning, I had a female student come up to me to say that she was feeling nauseous. She thought she was going to vomit. Of course, I said that she could go to the office to call home. My heart went out to her. I knew that the stomach flu had been going around in Calgary. There were many sick teachers and children who had caught this bug. I was a little concerned as I thought the child had got the stomach flu.

The little girl never came back to the class, so I assumed all was well. A short while after another child came to me and said that she was not feeling well. I thought, "My goodness – the bug is really going around." I again phoned the office to let them know that there was another child who was not feeling well.

The day before I had watched a video in a home economics class showing a church in Saskatchewan where the parishioners got sick from eating turkey. The turkey had not been cooked properly. I was in charge of my Christmas dinner at the church in Calgary, so I took great notice of this incident where many parishioners had fallen sick.

I still had not heard from the office when another child came to me to say she was not feeling well. I sent her to the office. I had four children who said they were not well. The assistant principal came in to tell me the children were fine. I felt a bit of a fool!

Discipline Issues
Mara Ganten

When you are a substitute teacher you enter every classroom knowing that students are not going to behave for you as they would for their own teachers. Let's face it; even good kids can act up when the "real teacher" is gone.

It even starts as young as Grade 1. I had a student who was messing around while he was supposed to be writing the daily message from the board onto a piece of paper. The message was along the lines of: Today is Monday, January 6, 2014. Bring your home reading and your skates for skating tomorrow.

If you know anything about Grade 1, you will know this task will take students anywhere from ten to thirty minutes to copy down off the board. If students don't finish it in the allotted time, they will stay in to finish it at recess or miss out on some free time, etc. Well, this one little student just couldn't settle down. He was talking and up and out of his seat all the time. I kept having to sit with him so he would stay still and write a letter or two.

I finally told him he would stay in for lunchtime recess to finish this if he didn't focus and do it now! His immediate response was, "Well, you aren't going to be here this afternoon, so I am NOT staying in."

Well, I'll tell you, he was a smart one! I wasn't going to be there that afternoon so there would be no way I could make him stay. However, what students don't know is that we teachers have our own tricks up our sleeves.

"Well," I said, "I happen to know your teacher very well. I will leave her a note and then call her this afternoon to make sure she keeps you in and you don't get your free time until you are done with your morning message." You could just see all the resistance slowly drain from his little body.

"Fine, I'll do it now!" he grumbled at me.

I smiled at him and said, "That is a great choice. Now I can let your teacher know how well you did this morning and how hard you worked to get your message done."

He finished his morning message smiling because he knew I was going to leave his teacher a nice message about him. I had a huge smile on my face as well because, although he wasn't happy to start with, he finished his work with a smile on his face! This is a good reminder that, as a teacher, you must celebrate even the small victories!

I am a Sub Sandwich!
Valsa Peter

When I walk into a class, kids yell out, "We have a sub!"

I tell them, "Yes, I am a Sub Sandwich with many fillings!"

As I start the lesson and we talk, I draw on the whiteboard.

Depending on the grade – let's say Grade 4– we pick out the subjects: English, Social Studies, Math, Phys Ed, Arts, ... Then I point out the Life Character Traits: Life Skills, Social Skills, Skits, Songs, Making Friends, ... After that, I get each kid to pick one Character Trait and write a paragraph or draw a picture of what that particular trait is and the impact on their life. This is my Sub Sandwich lesson!

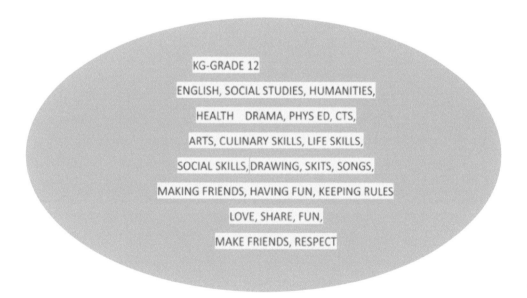

I am in love with teaching! My teaching past includes twenty years of international teaching and thirteen years with the Calgary Board of Education as a Substitute Teacher.

What gets me excited about going to work? Giving my all, as long as I can. Thirty-plus years and still going strong. It keeps me young at heart to walk into a classroom full of youngsters, full of life, questions, fun, laughter, pranks, and so on.

Grade 1 Joey: "You are a grandma! Grandmas don't teach; they bake pies!"
Me: "This grandma can teach and bake pies!"

Grade 2 Teacher: "Where is your assignment, Lucy? Did you read the deadline? Today is March 21."
Lucy: "Yes, I know... but the Sub did not write the year!"

Grade 12 Science: Chemistry is a Mystery with a History = Spelling and Pronunciation

I am surrounded by love. I celebrate milestones, birthdays, and Canada Day. I create lasting memories, get to teach, have *aha* moments, experience exciting days every day, and ignite the "spark!" I am a substitute with many fillings – kindergarten to Grade 12. Throw me in anywhere and I'll come up with special fragrances! My motto: *Substitute teaching is a work of the Heart!*

3

KIDS WILL BE KIDS

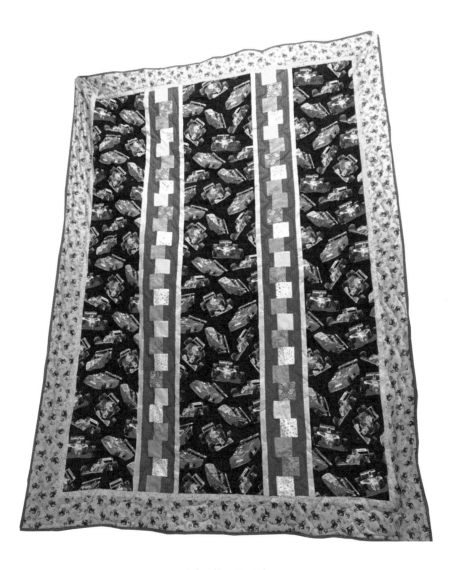

Abel's Quilt
Marcia Hicks

I made this quilt of racing cars for my great-nephew who was seven years old at the time. He loves the quilt and says it keeps him warm.

Your Name Please?
Shirley Ewing

As a teacher, kids have all kinds of games they will play with you. As a substitute teacher, you have fewer advantages for some of these. I used to say that you have to learn to play the games and win.

Not knowing students' names is always a challenge, but there are ways of getting around even this, if you are very observant. Seating plans, of course, are helpful. Many teachers make students write their names on a sign-out list to be excused to the washroom during a class. It is always possible to initiate sign-out sheets of your own, if necessary. Most students have their names on enough of their belongings that sometimes you can spot it at the right moment as you circulate around the room. Asking students to hand in their work, or just write their name on it at the beginning of the class, can also help. However, despite the best efforts you may put in, it can still be challenging to have the right name on hand for the right situation.

In one school, students took great pleasure in trying to confuse me by trading desks, trading names, or just giving me a name that didn't belong to anyone in the class. After a while, I started to get wise to this and began to think ahead, as to what might be the game of the day. One day, I decided to pay extra close attention as students came through the door, and it soon became one of my most valuable tools.

I discovered that as the students entered the room, they chatted casually with each other, occasionally using one another's names. I caught a couple of the names and tried to take note of the faces that were connected to them as students addressed other students.

Students took whatever seat they chose, even though I could not be sure if they were the right ones or not. After restating some classroom expectations, such as that students should raise their hands to speak and only one person should speak at a time, students tested me to see what they could get away with.

Asking a question of the class, I watched as some students were paying attention and others were not. Then I looked at the only person whose name I knew with any degree of certainty and confidently asked them for the answer, addressing them by name. The class fell silent, and all eyes were fixed on me as each student hesitantly questioned whether I knew their name as well. Of course, none of them needed to know who was known and who was not, nor how I had come into possession of the one name I had used.

On that day in a class in Northern Alberta, I gained an advantage and won the game.

She's My Cousin
Bunny Chan

I had been working as a substitute teacher for a couple of years with the Edmonton Public School Board (EPSB). The school district has around 200 schools consisting of elementary, junior high and high school sites.

My family is relatively small. At the time, I had one male cousin in the district as a student, but I was not aware of what school he was attending, nor was I privileged to know which teachers he had.

I was subbing for a social class one day at a high school. The second class was again a social class. My cousin came in and, although we were not close, we did recognize each other, and the class started. Attendance was taken and the assignment for the class was given. There was no seating plan and students were pretty respectful.

One student came in late. When I asked him what his name was, without hesitation, he gave me my cousin's name.

Without missing a beat, I called him out and replied, "No, it is not."

The student was adamant about it and proceeded to insist that this was his name. I played along but kept pressing him.

That is when my cousin leaned back and whispered to this individual, "She's my cousin."

We both got a laugh out of the story and the tardy student was no longer a problem.

I don't remember returning to this school, nor did I sub in my cousin's class again. In such a large district, what are the chances of connecting with my cousin, in that class, with this student impersonating him? One in a million. If I could only know the names of all my students.

My Most Significant Subbing Day
Jane Nieuwenhuis

Early one school morning, I received a call to sub at Calgary Christian High School! I was amazed as I consider myself exclusively an elementary teacher, but that just showed the desperation of the caller. I very reluctantly said, "Yes," and went to the school.

My first class was a combined "Homeroom" with about *seventy* Grade 12 students. The teacher had written, "Richard will take this."

Richard had crossed that out and written, "No. I won't. I am away to Kananaskis for an all-day field trip! Here is a video on inclusion."

The video was *fifteen* minutes long and had *three* discussion questions on the cover… for a *forty-five-minute* class.

My first issue was getting the video to play. After I fumbled around with the old TV and VCR in front of all those tech-savvy kids, a nice young man came up and helped me out. The video spoke about the inclusion of special needs students in the "normal" classroom. The first question listed was: What do you think of the inclusion of special needs students in your classroom?"

Out of the seventy students, one young lady put up her hand and replied, "I think it's nice."

Nice? That's it? End of discussion. No one else said a word. Not even after I threw out the next two questions. How was I to fill the rest of the forty-minute class? I had *no* idea what to do with all these Grade 12 students! Thankfully, the principal rescued me by showing up at that time and spoke to the kids about beginning their university applications.

When I got to the lunchroom at coffee break time, the English teacher heard my woeful tale and said, "Ahhh, Jane, you need to have a back pocket full of "tricks!" Just say, "I feel an essay coming on." They'll talk!"

Another eventful class that day was Grade 10 Social (for the teacher who was away on the field trip). When I welcomed the students to the class and gave them their assignment, most of them suddenly stood up and said, "We can study wherever we want," and left the room, despite my objections. Only a few students remained to work on their assignments in the classroom. Again, I had *no* idea what to do since the students had scattered themselves around the school and outdoors! This time, I hoped the principal would not show up!

I also had to teach a couple of sessions of CALM (Career and Life Management). The topic for the day was "troth," a seldom-used word for faithfulness and commitment in marriage. Part of the lesson included scenarios with dilemmas in them. For example, 23-year-old John wanted to get married as soon as 18-year-old Mary was done Grade 12. She wanted to travel and possibly study once high school was finished, even though she did love John. What should they do?

It was a much smaller class of about fifteen students, but this time discussion was not hard to come by. The group was clearly divided in their opinions, with half of the class siding with the young woman in the scenario, and half siding with the man.

The heated discussion went on for some time until one male student turned to me and asked, "How's YOUR marriage, Mrs. Nieuwenhuis?"

I was totally taken aback by the pointed questions and fumbled an evasive answer!
I was *soooo* relieved when the final bell rang that day. I have subbed many times, but this is the only subbing experience that left an indelible mark on my psyche. I think I'll stick with elementary children.

Just a Sec
May-Britt Mykietiak

When I first moved to Red Deer twenty years ago, I decided to sub for a year before seeking full-time employment. I accepted a three-day job for a Grade 2 teacher.

One little boy in the class had a habit of saying "Just a sec" every time I tried to redirect him.

By day three I was totally frustrated with hearing "Just a sec," so I shouted out, "No more secs," and added, "or minutes, or days, or…" when I realized I was facing a bunch of seven-year-olds, who were giggling behind their hands.

Did That Just Happen?
Mara Ganten

While I was filling in for someone on a temporary contract, I had to deal with a student who was well known for presenting challenging behaviours. As a matter of fact, this student had already been kicked out of the school and sent to alternate schooling. She was not supposed to be on the school campus.

One day, there were five minutes left in class and there was a knock at the art room door. A student goes to answer the door and in comes this girl who was suspended. At the time, I didn't know who she was or why she was there. She started to run around the room and shove things off the tables and onto the floor. She ran around the room destroying it while I literally chased after her asking her to stop. She actually stopped at one point and said aloud, "But there is nothing else for me to knock over." Then she ran out the door. I was not sure to whom she was talking.

The bell rang. I called the office to let them know that this student was loose in the building and told the students not to pick anything up because she would be coming back to clean it up! The kids just stood there shocked. One kid said, "That was *sooo* rude."

I let them all go and stared at the chaotic room, as tears slowly rolled down my cheek. I left the room, as it was, to clean up later. I normally wouldn't cry. I was just so frustrated and shocked that anyone could act in such a destructive manner.

After about ten minutes, I realized there would be no chance they would be able to track her down and actually make her clean anything up. I cleaned everything up so the next class didn't have to deal with it and then let the other art teacher know to keep his eye out for the student. For the next few days, I guarded my door like a hawk to make sure no one accidentally let the student in again.

Of course, my diligence was for nothing. I had been guarding the door all day and there were, again, five minutes of class left. Someone knocked on the door and a student got up to answer it before I could get there. The same student runs into the classroom. At this point, I am already making my way toward her to stop her from coming in, but she literally runs away as she is throwing anything she can. It was like a chase scene from the movies – things were flying throughout the room; desks and chairs were crashing over. The other students were frantically heading towards the doors hoping for the bell to ring so they could escape the chaos.

As if things couldn't get worse, the student runs to the phone and starts dialling. As I'm running to the phone, I hear students saying, "She's calling 911…. I think she's calling 911."

I ran to her, grabbed the phone out of her hand and hung up. She had the nerve to turn to me and say, "What are you doing?"

I couldn't even believe it. What was I doing? What was she doing? I looked her straight in the face and said, "Get out of this classroom immediately!"

She took off running down the hall. I called the office and they sent out a search party. She was caught and escorted off campus by the police.

I never did see her again (thank goodness), probably because she would be arrested the next time she set foot on campus. The administration apologized profusely as teachers really should not have to guard their doors. But I don't blame the administration; they had already taken the necessary steps and had her removed from the school. How were they to know that she really, really wanted to come back to terrorize the school? Although this was traumatizing, I do recognize this was a huge cry for help. I really hope she receives the help she so clearly needs.

What's in Your Coffee?
Marcheta Titterington

As I sit at the teacher's desk,
Looking at my plans for the day,
I savour my coffee
And won't let it stray!

I remember one winter morning going to an elementary school for a class that included Grade 5 and Grade 6 students. I had been at the school before for other classes, so I knew that their learning would be self-directed.

The teacher met me in the classroom when I arrived and shared with me her scheduled plans for the day, before leaving. When it was time for science that day, she showed me different containers of solutions that the students would be mixing. These were located on a low shelf accessible to all and the students would know what to do.

The morning went quite well that day but, just before recess, it was time for science. The grade five and six students went about mixing their solutions and recording needed information about their experiments.

At recess, I didn't notice anything unusual happening. When all the students went outside, I made my way to the staff room and then realized I had left my coffee behind. I made my way back to the classroom before the bell rang, signalling that recess would soon be over.

When I arrived back in the classroom, a young girl was waiting there to talk with me. She told me how some of the students had taken all the teacher's pens outside and hidden them in the snow. It was to look like I had taken the teacher's pens! The young student went on to say that one of the boys thought it would be funny to see what would happen to me when I drank my coffee. Apparently, their science experiments ended up in my coffee. I thanked her for kindly letting me know and I was glad that I hadn't touched my coffee. I received many sorry notes after that day.

Later, when I was telling my cousin Anne, a substitute teacher also, she told me that students had once put staples in her coffee. A word to the wise -

As you savour your coffee
Like you always do
When it's recess or lunchtime,
Please take it with you.

Poetry to be sung to a well-known spaghetti song.

Teenage Boy Weightlifting
Mara Ganten

One day, I was subbing in a Grade 11 physical education class; we were going to be working with the weights for the period. We all know the group of students that gathers during gym period and basically attempts to avoid participating. I am fully aware of this group because I was one of those students when I was in high school! I can relate to and identify with them.

I always try to motivate those groups of students into participating in the class. I walked over to the group of students, which mostly consisted of girls, and started chatting them up, while I was using three-to-five-pound weights and doing some arm curls. I finally got them doing squats and lunges with light weights. As we were working out, they started to explain why they really hated working in the weight room as much as they do. It's not because they don't like using weights or working out; it's because some of the boys insist on acting like they are champion weightlifters and like to make a big scene. The girls explained how annoying and immature it was to watch the boys try and show off their "skills." One girl pointed to a group of boys and said, "See! This is what we are talking about."

I looked over to see one tall boy attempting to lift a rather heavy bar. All his friends were crowding around him and cheering him on. This boy was grunting and huffing and pulling and really making a scene, so more people were coming over to watch the spectacle. I looked over at the group of girls and they had this look on their faces that clearly said, "Seriously! This is what we have to deal with all the time," while they rolled their eyes at the boys.

Now that the boy had his audience, he really started getting serious. He decided to grab a weight belt (yes, like the ones you see in actual weight-lifting competitions) and he put chalk on his hands. He told everyone to be quiet because he needed silence to do this. Again, I looked at the girls and got the eye roll. I couldn't even look at the girls without laughing now because they were just so unimpressed with this whole thing. The rest of the class was now watching the boy try to lift this weight.

On his first attempt, he lifted the bar maybe two centimetres off the floor. Then he told the kids to make a bit of noise to pump him up for his next attempt. Again, I glanced at the girls, and I cracked up because they looked exasperated! All the kids started cheering and pumping this kid up. He started grunting and huffing and this time lifted the bar about a foot off the ground. I was silently laughing to myself at his failed attempts, while the rest of the class was cheering him on for the amazing job he did (really…amazing?). I looked at the girls and they were still super unimpressed. Then the boy was done with his show for the day, telling everyone that the last lift really took a lot out of him.

The girls came over to me and one said, "You see what we have to deal with all the time?" I agreed. I definitely felt for them having to watch this "feat." I think I burned more calories laughing during the period than our champion weightlifter did.

The Physics Exam
Bev Maertens-Poole

Many years ago, I substituted at Camrose Composite High School in Camrose. Sometimes it was in a subject area in which I had absolutely no experience. I didn't even choose physics in high school. Dr. Ram taught physics and was away. He prepared an exam for me to administer. After class, I picked up this piece of paper. I am sure the two students (boys) never did very well on the exam.

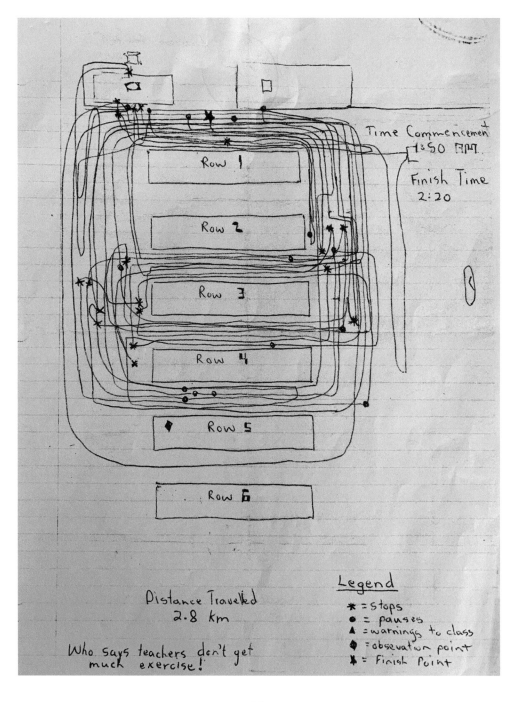

4

CONNECTIONS

Turn Around and Find the Flow
Kathy Cook

Although I love to illustrate many things in nature, magpies are one of my favourite subjects. Like many people, before I began drawing magpies, I found them to be bothersome. No doubt they are plentiful, loud, and aggressive. One day, I decided to embrace what is awesome about these birds, instead of letting myself feel annoyed with their presence. It was like a veil of negativity was lifted and suddenly their unique qualities became clear. I began to look forward to seeing these beautiful, resilient, intelligent birds. In many ways, this reminds me of working with students who present as high-needs learners. If you look past the challenging behaviours of students who are frustrated due to learning disabilities, problems with emotional regulations and/or very difficult home situations, you are more able to see their positive qualities. Many of these students, given the chance, reveal unique, creative, sensitive, and loving natures. Over the years, I truly began to look forward to working with the more complex learners. I can honestly say that I have learned as much from them as they have from me.

The Good, The Bad and The In-Between
Karen Williams

As I sit down to write this memoir, I think to myself: Are my memories good ones? Are my memories bad ones? Are my memories between the two opposite sides of the scale? After thirty years of substitute teaching and temporary contracts, what do I take away from the moments and the days of substitute teaching?

My first good memories are of the students – the nice ones, the kind ones, the remarkable students who go out of their way and ask, "Mrs. Williams, can I help you find the book, the library cards, the papers you are looking for?" The lovely students who at the end of the day say, "Thank you, Mrs. Williams. I hope we see you again. Are you coming back tomorrow?" I treasure the creative, giving students who have given me pictures they have drawn during the day for me to keep. I treasure the notes and cards they have given me. I have kept many of those keepsakes in a special file and many of the pictures have been on a magnet on our fridge in the kitchen for periods of time. Those are my heartfelt memories.

My second set of memories is of the difficult moments that I have tried to laugh away. There are moments such as issues with attendance. There are moments of not knowing what is waiting or what the day may hold. There was the day I tripped over something in the classroom and landed splat down like an elephant as I took down a couple of grade-one chairs along the way. There was the day I was knocked down flat by a ball in the gym. A bunch of the grade-two students ran to the office to tell them I was dead. Eventually, I surprised everyone by standing up stunned and dazed.

In-between memories are ones of trying to find the school in the morning darkness. There are memories of driving and arriving at the school during frigidly cold winter days and hoping that someone was in the school who could open the door to let me inside. I started my very first substitute teaching job with a ticket for an illegal U-turn, as I was frantically trying to find the school and had gone the wrong way. I also have a memory of one day leaving my car in the school parking lot to come out at the end of the day and find a flat tire. Did a student do it or, in my constant struggle with the students that day, was it only my imagination that a student would flatten my tire? I remember doing a lot of supervision until the board policy came through that a substitute teacher doesn't have to supervise until lunch break. I remember students bursting with energy and how nice it was to come home and have a cup of tea at the end of the day.

Being actively part of the Alberta Teachers' Association (ATA) and being a part of the Calgary Substitute Teachers' Group (STG) has enhanced my substitute teaching experience. The friendships I have formed I hope will last forever. In the STG of the ATA, we have all tried to make the substitute teaching job a little easier. My dad was involved with the transit union and the one thing he requested of me, as he and my mom were putting me through university, was that somewhere along the way I get involved and do some work for the teachers' association. So, I hope I have honoured you in doing that, Dad.

Now, as I get older, students are starting to ask, "Are you the teacher's mom?" "Whose grandma, are you?" I will take my cue from the students and will start to think about retirement. I am writing these final words as I am on a summer holiday looking over one of the beautiful lakes in the Okanagan. Substitute teaching has not been a very conventional job, but it has given me opportunities to smile, to laugh, to cry, to learn. At the end of it all, from all my days of substitute teaching, a touch of the old teaching magic will linger inside me and will always be part of my soul!

The Bright Red Runners
Linda Klym

I was doing a long-term stint for a Grade 6 teacher. She told me there was one young man who refused to put on his running shoes, or any shoes, for that matter. She asked him daily, but somehow he got away with wearing his socks around the school.

I decided to approach this problem with a different tactic. I was not going to ask the student to put on his shoes, as that was exactly what he wanted me to do. I ignored the shoe issue for a good week, even though it really did bug me that he was breaking school policy.

One day, after all the students left, I put little notes in the shoes. One note said, "I'm so lonely!" The other note said, "Why doesn't anyone want me?"

The next day, I pretended to ignore the morning rituals the students did as they arrived. I had to go to another class right after taking the register. When I returned to my homeroom, the red runners were on the feet of this student, and he wore them for the rest of my time in the classroom. I never said a word to anyone, nor did he! It was our own private little joke. It was moments like this that made me love being a substitute teacher.

My Embarrassing Teaching Moment That Got Me a Job
Karen McKenzieSmith

What! Even the Substitute Teaching Roster was frozen! Now, what was I going to do?

I couldn't even get near the Human Resources Department of the CBE, Public School District in Calgary. A colleague of mine suggested I go straight to the top. She knew the superintendent in charge at the time. She suggested that I speak to this person directly. So, I did! All I wanted was for somebody to hear me out. After it was all said and done, I was actually able to speak to the head of the Human Resources Department after all.

This is what happened.

When I went for my interview, he kept saying, "You realize, this will not get you a job."

It was a behavioural-type interview, which I like the most. So that was a relief! Hence, he started off by asking me what was the most embarrassing teaching moment I had experienced. It didn't take more than a second for me to recall such an embarrassing teaching moment in my career as a teacher.

It was a time when I was teaching kindergarten. I was teaching the topic of "community." I had a great idea to make an ant farm. So, I gathered some ants from an ant hill I located. Thinking I should include some more ants, I found another ant hill to raid and collect. Perfect, I thought, as I displayed my ant farm so admirably in a special spot in the classroom. Then I gathered the children together. As I started to teach about community, relating it to the ant farm I had shown the children, one lone child noticed something odd and exclaimed in a troubled tone, "Teacher, why is there only one alone ant I can see hobbling around looking wounded?"

Oh, my Lord! It did not dawn on me at the time that you absolutely cannot put two different ant colonies together in one place or they will fight to the death! (How could I possibly talk about community now? Not when all the ants were dead but one. That is not community! Oh, ohhh, oops!)

So, I solved the problem by talking about the opposite of community….which can turn out to be war!

The head of Human Resources started laughing so hard that he excused himself and left the office, returning not too long after with a bunch of forms for me to fill out. As he handed me the forms, he stated that I would be able to start the following week.

I got the job!

Making a Difference
Anne Deeves

The best experience any substitute teacher can have is when one is able to really connect with a student and see amazing results. Such a case for me was Dougie, a grade-four student who had totally "fallen through the cracks", as the saying goes. Dougie was simply scribbling on each line on the page, yet all his pages had been stamped "Good".

I started an individual program with him and a home program for him to do with help from his mom. Gradually, Dougie began to read and write. I knew Dougie until he went to high school where he was successful in Math 14 and could read and write well enough to do the program.

I have had so many memorable experiences! One time, I bought party dresses for two little girls in my sister's Early Childhood Services class so that they would attend the class Christmas concert and Sharing Day.

Sadly, sometimes things go wrong. Once, at 7:00 a.m., my sister answered our phone and a teacher I had substituted for the day before started yelling at her. "How dare you open my cupboard and allow the students to use my books! These students are liars and thieves, they won't return the books."

There was not a lesson plan available that day. The students assured me that they were supposed to start some new books. In any case, I went to Chapters and bought a few books with the same titles to replace any of the teacher's books that might be missing. Fortunately, most teachers do not behave like that. The majority of teachers that I worked for were always appreciative of my efforts to teach their students.

Sometimes, problems arise dealing with students and occasionally a situation becomes dangerous. At one junior high school, I was robbed and threatened. I was afraid to go to the parking lot to get my car to go home. I actually phoned my nephew, a young man who is 6'2", and 180 pounds. When he arrived and the culprits saw him with me, they decided against their actions and took off! Fortunately, the majority of students are not like them.

Over the years, teaching students within the Calgary Board of Education has been a wonderful privilege.

Real Life Learning
Mara Ganten

For a few months, I was filling in for a teacher who was on medical leave, and I was teaching Abnormal and Personal Psychology to thirty-seven Grade 11 and 12 students. I know what you are thinking. Thirty-seven students! However, this was an elective course, so everyone chose to be there. There were no behaviour issues, just a lot of marking!

My classroom was located near our special education classrooms. We had a new student with autism join our program that year. When he would get excited, he would run up and down the hallways, yelling and screaming with excitement. He was a wonderfully happy student and I had no way to predict the huge impact he would have on my class that term.

I could visibly see that my students were uncomfortable with what society would consider to be "abnormal behaviour." When the student would go running through the halls, my students' body language would change, their facial expressions would change, and you could sense their discomfort. I knew this was the perfect learning environment and opportunity for a real-world learning experience.

We talked about how "normal human behaviour" is what the majority of society considers "acceptable behaviour," and "abnormal human behaviour" is anything that doesn't fall into that category. Why does abnormal behaviour make people uncomfortable? Well, it is because most people don't know how to react to abnormal behaviour, so they feel at a loss as to how to respond and that makes them uncomfortable.

I knew this student from previously substituting in his class before I was filling in for the medical leave at the school. His teacher and I discussed having him come in to slowly introduce himself to us. At that time, he was using an iPad to communicate with us. He started out coming into our classroom with his educational assistant (EA) to say hello. He would come in with a huge smile and press "Hello" on the iPad and we would all respond. He would giggle and scream in excitement, which initially made some students uncomfortable. After a while, he was able to have a short conversation using his iPad and we would cheer, clap, get really excited, and we would all celebrate his achievements. You could slowly see my students start opening up and becoming more comfortable with different behaviours.

When he was more comfortable, he would come in and tell us a joke using his iPad, which we all enjoyed. Again, the class would respond and cheer him on and thank him for coming to see us. My students started saying hello to this student throughout the day, instead of just during our classes. They were much more comfortable. The student was also becoming more outgoing, and he started giving high fives in the hallway, which was great.

Approximately halfway through the second semester our special student finally started speaking verbally! His mom heard him call her "Mom" for the first time ever and this boy was fifteen years old! As you can imagine, his teacher, his EA, his mom, and I all cried in celebration! It was an amazing accomplishment! He started off the year nonverbal and not writing at all and he finished off the year being able to greet people, say goodbye, and have a short conversation. He was also writing simple sentences. Obviously, this student was finally receiving the help he needed to move forward. He had an amazing special education teacher and two wonderful educational assistants that helped him, plus a wonderful class of amazing individual students that helped cheer him on and make learning exciting.

Introducing this student to my Abnormal and Personal Psychology class provided an enriched learning experience for everyone involved. It provided the student with ASD (autism spectrum disorder) invaluable opportunities to interact socially with his peers. It also helped the class understand that abnormal behaviour isn't bad; it is different, which can lead to people feeling uncomfortable. This experience has reinforced the importance of taking time to understand one another and celebrate our differences. Those differences distinguish us as individuals and make the world a more interesting place.

Through this learning experience, the class was able to explore and observe "abnormal behaviour" in a safe, risk-free environment. They learned that they shared more similarities with our student with autism than they initially realized. He just expresses himself in different ways, and once they were willing to learn how he expressed himself in what might be considered "abnormal" ways, beautiful and beneficial relationships emerged.

5

COVID-19

The COVID Quilt
Marcia Hicks

I made this quilt for my daughter, and she named it the "COVID Quilt." The pattern I used is called the "Monkey Wrench." See if you can find the block that is practicing *social distancing*.

A Moment in Time
Lee Nagy

This is overwhelming
I'm not getting things done
My heart is breaking
How do Nova Scotians cope?

The outlook looks bleak
My house is a mess
Which friends do I reach out to?
Which app do I use?

With all this time on our hands
How can I feel so lost?
Too many choices
I need a long pause

To get caught up
To get my house clean
To sort through old clothes

Today is much better
I awoke with a calm
Paper read, puzzles done
On to cleaning and yoga online.

One by one I'll get things done
Sort my mail, pay my bills,
Finish a book, write it down,
File away work, tidy the desk

Line up to shop, buy way too much,
Lug it home, sort it through
Repackage for meals, plan for weeks,
Never take my hubby with me again

Through My Kitchen Window – April 2020
Marcheta Titterington

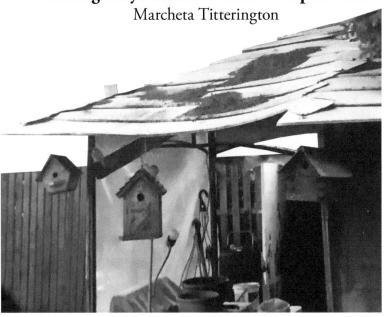

As I pause to look outside
Through my kitchen window
I see warm westerly winds
Are blowing and gently rocking
Our little weathered birdhouses
They are reminiscent
Of the many yesteryears,
Providing warmth, shelter,
And a new life for our sweetly
Chirping feathered friends
It's Springtime now.

Fresh green leaves have just
Burst out upon the branches
Of our trees
Even on our older tree
Bending low, almost touching
The ground, save for a smaller
Branch giving support,
Providing a cane
For its elderly friend.

In past months, I have been the
Traveling Music Teacher,

Pushing my trolley of
Musical materials
Through the hallways
Of many schools
Like the westerly wind
And like my elderly friend
The tree, for I am
A Great Grandmother now.

I miss the children and
The older students when
I'm not there.
I love being their teacher for
They have been my reward
Throughout all my years
Of teaching.
Like the newness of Spring.
But for now they are not at
School and neither am I.
Perhaps another week we'll be
Together again,
But we must wait and see.
It's Springtime now

COVID - March 2020
Penny Smith

COVID or Coronavirus seemed so far away when I first heard about it.
This was on cruise ships or found in China
Scary thoughts when WHO declared a pandemic on March 11th
Never in Calgary, so I thought
Scarier and scarier.
Subbed on March 13 – the last day of school – hallways packed with students.
Didn't hear the news that schools would close on Sunday night.
It was eerie quiet when I walked the dogs on Monday
No one at the bus stops on Monday March 16.
No traffic
Something was afoot
Heard a message on my phone that schools were closed
This is 2020 not 1917,
News got depressing about deaths – switched channels to get music on the radio.
The female disc jockey played Queen's "Another One Bites the Dust."
I just about fell through the floor on hearing that.
Depressing to hear about thousands of deaths,
When will this end?
Social distancing is a norm.
Waited on phone for four and a half hours to talk to a real person in EI
Never seen so many puppies in my life.
Every day, I came across new puppies at the dog park
Or walking around my neighbourhood
I have seen Tibetan Mastiffs, Golden Retrievers, Staffordshire Terriers, Labradors, German Shepherd
Puppies, Bernese Mountain Dogs
Dog people hope this is not a trend.
I talked to one owner who was going to Greece
But got a puppy instead.
Playing tennis and walking through the forests
And prairie grasses with my dog
Helps keep one in perspective.
Hopefully this nightmare will be over soon.

Penny with her dog, Spenser.

COVID – 19
Pansy Pilgrim

COVID - 19,
you have tried to penetrate
our society
But you will soon be stopped
by the Almighty
We think 2022 is too long to
wait for you to disappear
We hope and pray that you
Will not soon reappear

A COVID Prayer
Pansy Pilgrim

Continue to serve the Lord
Only believe in his word, which is its own reward
Rely on him for all your needs
Open your hearts and never cease to do good deeds
Never doubt that you are not alone in these troubling days
Almighty God you are our refuge and strength in this moment
And always
Virus, the one we serve will not let you overtake the earth
In you, O' Lord we find peace and joy as we rejoice in your birth
Reach out to the lonely, the sick, and the unbelieving
Under your protection we will be gladly receiving
Savior, we worship and adore you and continue to keep the faith we
Are achieving

River
Lucia Semenoff

as the ancient river flows
through this moment
calm, peaceful, green
I cross the bridge
leaving yesterday behind
slipping
into tomorrow

this river was here
before
so was the bridge, but I
I - was not

today
time is holding
my hand
with the unknown

April 2020

Spring 2020
Lucia Semenoff

I no longer hurry or rush
plan schedules
busy agendas
assignments –

Instead, I reflect slowly
as if stitching time
to a precious cloth
I watch birds
build nests
dive gracefully
with freedom

I pause –
evenings used to be
preparing for tomorrow
for now I am only in the
Moment

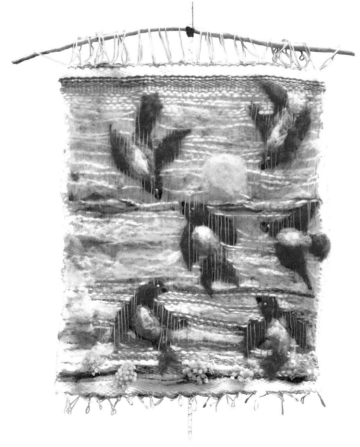

Pick Up the Pieces
Kathy Cook

Take a long slow breath
Step up to the light
Have the honesty to admit that something
Just ain't right
We all need a balance
In our lives just the same
If you don't learn your lesson
You're gonna get to do it all again and again

Cause maybe ....Oh maybe
You've gotta turn around pick up the pieces and move on
You've gotta turn around pick up the pieces and move on

Take a long slow breath
Step up take a chance
Do you hear the music
Leading you on into your own dance
Deep down inside your soul
You know which way to go
If life's become a struggle
You've gotta turn around and find your flow

Cause maybe ....Oh maybe
You've gotta turn around pick up the pieces and move on
You've gotta turn around pick up the pieces and move on

Take a long slow breath
Step up make a choice
Do you follow all the rest
Can you still hear your own voice
Take what seems a problem
Go to peace and find your strength
Oh change is gonna happen
If you live your life to any length, any length

Cause maybe ....Oh maybe
You've gotta turn around pick up the pieces and move on
You've gotta turn around pick up the pieces and move on

Check out Kathy Cook and her band, Magnolia Buckskin, on YouTube

Kathy Cook began writing "Pick Up the Pieces" while sitting alone in Linas's Market in NW Calgary, sipping hot chocolate and contemplating life's constant changes.

COVID has forced us to transform our understanding of education. As technology begins to take a major role in the delivery of teaching and learning, we are increasingly reminded of the great importance of human connection.

Life changes are inevitable. Whether positive, negative, predictable, or unpredictable, we are often forced to let go of the familiar and face new ways of dealing with day-to-day existence.

Flowers of Hope
Lucia Semenoff

I created this tapestry in the spring of 2020, at the beginning of our global pandemic. Like many others during the lockdown, I was wondering about uncertainty, different communities, and what comes next. My work reflects these thoughts and feelings.

As I was weaving recycled cotton and yarn, I visualized patience and hope. For me, hope comes in many forms. This work incorporates dried flower, as I often include elements of nature in my art practice. While the flowers integrated in my work are dry, they hold seeds for renewal – like spring – new growth and hope.

As an educator, I was thinking and continue to think about all the students and teachers during these trying times. There is a heart outlined in the centre of my artwork. It is a symbol of hope for the future of our children.

6

EPILOGUE

Alberta Teachers' Association
Anne Deeves

It was always a privilege to serve on the Substitute Teachers' Group (STG) Executive of Calgary Public Teachers (Local 38 of the Alberta Teachers' Association (ATA)), knowing that your service was helping substitute teachers in many ways. Substitutes need information, professional development, counselling, assistance with obtaining contracts, social experiences, and help with taking their concerns to the ATA and to the Calgary Board of Education (CBE). I enjoyed the work with colleagues and made many friends. The STG of the day realized that, because substitutes did not have a regular staff to be part of, our social agenda was of equal importance to the other professional aspects of the work of the committee. Our STG had an excellent relationship with people like Richard Hehr (Local 38), Karen de Massi (CBE), Jenny Regal (Local 38 President), Larry Liffiton (Local 38), Shannon Doherty (CBE Sub Desk) and many others. These people were always willing to help us and support us.

It was always wonderful to obtain temporary contracts over the years and to have the teaching/learning experience with the children that regular teachers experience every day. A few of the schools I served at were Louis Riel Elementary, Gordon Townsend (at the Alberta Children's Hospital), R.B. Bennett Elementary, Terry Fox Junior High, and Jack James Senior High. I even did some substituting at the Young Offenders Centre, where I heard some heartbreaking stories from the students.

I was also fortunate enough to have Shirley Smart as a sister and had the benefit of her knowledge from her many years of teaching in Early Childhood Education. As a retired teacher, she was always completely supportive of substitute teachers and took part in many of our STG activities. She always gave us good advice and helped us with our concerns. We were grateful when regular teachers cared about us and gave their support. They say, "Sometimes getting the job may be whom you know!" That may have been the case for me at one school because the principal knew Shirley and had worked with her for a few years.

Anne Deeves dictated this essay and the story titled "Making a Difference" to her sister, Shirley Smart, while Anne was in the hospice. She passed away shortly thereafter, on June 13, 2018.

Committee Members' Biographies

Marcheta Titterington

Marcheta grew up in Calgary, Alberta, after venturing west from Toronto with her mom and dad in 1947. She received her Bachelor of Education Degree from the University of Calgary and a Diploma in Early Childhood Education and Development from Mount Royal College. Marcheta has been teaching for the Calgary Board of Education for over 26 years and continues to be an active member of the ATA, notably serving on the Substitute Teachers' Group Executive, the Council of School Representatives and as a delegate to the ATA's Annual Representative Assembly. She has written articles and stories about travel and people, directed and produced plays, and has loved entertaining in Musical Theatre.

Penny Smith

Penny was born in England, close to Sherwood Forest, and she came to Canada aboard the ship Saxonia. Penny's first educational experience was in a school that her great grandfather started in Gringley-on-the-Hill. Penny has four degrees and, while at university and acting as the ARTS representative, she convinced city council to give bus passes to post-secondary students. Penny has worked as a journalist, in the oil patch and as a teacher to adult ESL students. She is currently a substitute teacher with the Calgary Board and is a Member-at-Large on the Substitute Teachers' Group (STG) Committee where she has served as chair and vice-chair for a number of years. Her hobbies include photography, bird watching, hiking, swimming, skiing and playing tennis. Penny enjoys taking her three Golden Retrievers on walks.

Karen Williams

Karen was born in Calgary, Alberta. She started her teaching career as a kindergarten and grade one teacher for 7 years in the Northern Lights School District in Bonnyville, Alberta. She has been a substitute teacher with the Calgary Board of Education since 1990 and has over 2000 substitute teaching days to her credit. She has been an active member of the ATA Substitute Teachers' Group and is currently the Past Chair. Karen enjoys reading, hiking and travelling. She has travelled to all seven continents in the world.

Marcia Hicks

Marcia received her Bachelor of Education from the University of British Columbia and her Diploma in Special Education from Thompson Rivers University. As a certificated teacher in both Alberta and British Columbia, she taught in a variety of settings such as rural to city. The vast majority of her career has been as a substitute teacher with assignments being varied: Business Education, Youth Detention Center, Adult Education, and Special Education.

Valsa Peter

Teaching is the only profession Valsa Peter has done!
Valsa graduated with professional teaching credentials in India and worked there for 10 years. She lived and worked in an Education related capacity for 22 years in Saudi Arabia for an international oil company. Then Valsa made her way to Canada. This is her last stop! Valsa is now employed with the Calgary Board of Education as a substitute teacher. She loves her job! Valsa finds it very fulfilling and satisfying!! Valsa says she is surrounded by love, celebrates milestones, birthdays, holidays! Her school days have created lasting memories, she gets to experience Ha Ha Moments, exciting days every day, igniting the 'spark'! Valsa's teaching motto: TEACHING COMES FROM THE HEART!!

Lee Nagy

Lee has a BSc and MSc in Physical Geography. She worked as the Executive Coordinator of the Alberta Association for Disabled Skiers prior to having two children and returning to university for her Education degree. Lee started her teaching career in the elementary division and retired in 2013 as a math, science, and special education teacher at the junior high level. Since then, she has been enjoying the varied work of a substitute teacher and is currently a member of the Calgary Substitute Teachers' Group. Lee enjoys sports, puzzles, reading and spending time with family.

Consulting Editor

Robert Benner is a graduate of the University of Calgary where he graduated with a B.A. in Religious Studies and received his B.Ed. from the University of Alberta. He has been with the CBE since 1997. Robert has subbed and had temporary contracts in many high schools throughout the CBE. He is currently a permanent teacher at Nelson Mandela High School, where he has taught English since 2016.

Authors' Biographies

James Baker has been a kindergarten to grade 12 substitute and contracted teacher for the Calgary Board of Education and Rocky View School Board over the past 24 years. He is heavily involved with Local 38 of the ATA with years serving on the STG Executive, the Local 38 Executive, the Council of School Representatives, the Teacher Welfare Committee, and as a delegate to the to the Annual Representative Assembly of the ATA. James is currently the Chair of the STG Directorate. He has volunteered with several nature organizations in the Calgary area, such as the Calgary Zoo and the Inglewood Bird Sanctuary.

Bunny Chan has had a teaching career with the Edmonton Public School Board. She spent a few years working as a substitute teacher, going to various elementary, junior high and high school sites in the district.

Kathy Cook has enjoyed being involved in teaching for almost three decades. She has vast experience as a homeroom academic educator, as well as a music and art specialist. When she is not teaching, you will likely see her playing music with her band *Magnolia Buckskin* or out hiking somewhere in the great Canadian Rockies.

Anne Deeves was an Abel Seaman from 1967 to 1969 in the Royal Canadian Naval Reserve at HMCS Tecumseh in Calgary, sharing many adventures with her husband, Alec. After attaining her PMLA (Petroleum, Mineral & Land Administration) diploma from Mount Royal College, she worked in the oil industry for many years. In the 1980's, she attended the University of Calgary, attaining her BA in English and her B.Ed. Anne was a dedicated substitute teacher from 1988-2017. She was always an enthusiastic participant in the Substitute Teachers' Group and the Alberta Teachers' Association, working diligently on behalf of substitute teachers. Anne passed away peacefully on June 13, 2018, at Dulcina Hospice in Calgary and she dictated her contribution to this book while she was there.

Shirley Ewing, having grown up on an Alberta farm, spent most of her teaching career as a substitute. Her early teaching years were in the Valley View area of Alberta, East of Grande Prairie, then a year in Papua, New Guinea, followed by teaching in a charter school in Calgary and then joining the Calgary Board of Education. She enjoyed all school ages but spent most of her time in JHS and SHS.

Her areas were Foods and Fashion. Subbing is not a temporary occupation for her. It is a position she has chosen to be in for a significant time.

Mara Ganten was born and raised in the beautiful mountain town of Revelstoke. She graduated from the University of Alberta in 2007 with a B.Ed. Mara is currently working for Edmonton Public Schools. She was a substitute for about 9 years with temporary contracts. She was actually planning on writing her own book about subbing, but that fell by the wayside! She read about this opportunity in the ATA newsletter. She has a collection of funny, serious and touching stories. She also has a collection of typical things you hear kids say about subs or to subs!

Linda Klym was born in Edmonton, Alberta and did most of her teaching and all of her subbing in Sherwood Park. She was in the teaching profession from 1972 to 2014 in one way or another. Linda now lives in Vernon, British Columbia, but Alberta will always be her home.

Bev Maertens-Poole lives in Camrose, Alberta with her husband of 60 years, Bill. She grew up on a farm north of Hughenden. After graduation from high school, she began teacher training at the University of Alberta with the aid of a bursary from the local School Division. Her teaching career began in Provost, Alberta, where she met Bill who joined the staff. The family moved to Camrose in 1967. There are three children and four grandchildren who faithfully include the "old folks" in their lives.

Karen McKenzieSmith was born in Saskatchewan near Cypress Hills and has lived in Alberta for over 61 years, raising her three children. She received a Diploma in Early Childhood Services from the University of Lethbridge and a B Ed (Double Major) in Elementary Math/Social from the University of Alberta. Karen began her teaching career in Lethbridge and Magrath, Alberta, and in later years taught as a Substitute Teacher for the Calgary Board of Education and the Calgary Catholic School Board. She was an active member of the ATA, serving as Chair of the Substitute Teachers' Group, and established Grid Pay for Substitute Teachers in Alberta. She has served on a number of community boards and has received many awards in art, writing, poetry, public speaking, and even a gold medal in Mixed Curling in Japan. She is a best-selling author of several books.

May-Britt Mykietiak taught as a substitute teacher for a year when she first moved to Red Deer over twenty years ago. She continued to teach as a full-time teacher thereafter.

Jane Nieuwenhuis stayed home for 14 years to raise her four children, after teaching for 7 years (1999-2006). She did have her name on the subbing list at Calgary Christian School for many of those years that she stayed home and later became a contract teacher there for nineteen years and for four years at Heritage Christian School. Her three grandchildren fill her life now.

Pansy Pilgrim has been a teacher for the Calgary Board of Education for the past number of years. She is an active member of the ATA, serving as Secretary of the Substitute Teachers' Group Executive. The highlight of her teaching career is writing skits, songs, and poems for a variety of events and performing them in front of a live audience.

Lucia Semenoff has roots in Russia, Chile, Finland and Canada. She holds a BFA from Alberta College of Art and Design and a B.Ed. from the University of Calgary and has been teaching with the Calgary Board of Education since 2012. Lucia has a passion for hiking in nature, writing and art-making. She also loves spending time with her family and friends. Gardening and cooking meals together with her husband and four adult children are Lucia's most enjoyable activities.

Roger Scott is presently a retired 40+ year teacher/coach/administrator living the "good life" with his patient and adoring wife, Ann, in St. Albert, Alberta. A proud Physical Education Grad (U of A '73) and lifetime HPEC'r, Roger attained his PDAD in '74 and his MEd (UVic '82). He has taught, coached, and administrated in six St. Albert Public Schools, retiring as Principal and Assistant Principal at Lorne Akins Jr. High in 2014. Roger subbed and coached from his retirement until COVID in 2020 and hopes to re-commence work with 'Gatorugby' this spring, 2022. His enjoyment of writing was honed through the benefit of strong teaching influences at Glenora, Westminster, and Ross Sheppard Schools.

Joyce Verrier grew up on a small farm in northern Alberta during the 1940s and '50s. Money was scarce and times were tough. Mother often said, "If only I had a way to become a teacher, ..." That would have been a cure-all for her. I'm glad I took the hint from her because, at almost 80 years of age, I am still enjoying the wonders of teaching. What a great life!

Looking to the Future

We all have stories to tell about subbing in Alberta. It is our hope that someday those who come after us will embark on a journey like we did and publish another very special book of stories and poems, written from the heart, by substitute teachers from all over Alberta.

Printed in the United States
by Baker & Taylor Publisher Services